Nothing Says a

Good Day Like a

DIVORCE...

If You Prepare for it!

What Divorce Attorneys Won't Tell You

A Step-by-Step Guide to Preparing for Divorce

Helen M. Dukhan, Esq., LL.M.

COPYRIGHT

DEDICATION

To all of those soon beginning a new chapter of their life. Be strong, be brave, be sensible, be you.

— Remember to Breath–
It Won't Always Be This Hard

ACKNOWLEDGEMENTS

Before we start, I just want to mention those individuals who you and I should thank for making this book possible. I would like to thank, first and foremost, my husband, Ilan, for his patience, constant support, and unsolicited and solicited advice; my two boys, S & N, for providing me with cuddles, laughs, and distractions when I needed it most during the writing process; my assistant Amy Griffith for reading the manuscript, giving me great feedback, and for all her hard work running my law office and handling my day to day tasks, ultimately allowing me time to write and get this book completed; my editor, Russel Womack, for his professionalism, skill, feedback, responsiveness, and for taking a true interest in my work; my cover designer, Noel Sellon, for taking my embarrassing designs and turning them into "gold" – literally!; Eric Robinson, for his hard work formatting and designing the inside body of my book for print and for ebook. His patience is unparalleled!; my muse, one of my closest friends and trusted advisor, Dalia Lightman, founder of Story of Life Therapy and Story of Life Photography, for taking the photo of me that graces the cover of this book, for your friendship, for allowing me to sit on your couch whenever necessary (both literally and figuratively), and for reviewing this guide and, as always, giving me honest and thoughtful feedback; my friend and amazing photographer, Jean Terman, founder of Jean Terman Photography, for taking my professional headshot used in the book and, by doing so, empowering me every time I look at it. Also, I can't forget the ladies who provided me with advice upon demand, Dominique Lauten and Allison Mentzel. Dominique, I must also thank you for reading the entire guide and providing me with your edits and hilarious commentary!

I also want to thank my parents, Irina and Mikhail Dukhan, my big brother, Dmitry Dukhan, and my grandparents, Sofia and Semyon Kazakov, for their constant support. They taught me that I can do anything I set my mind to. My dedushka never went a day of his life without writing in his journal and continues to inspire me with his wisdom, strength and desire to help others.

Last, but not least, I must thank all of my clients that I have had the privilege to represent. I have been able to learn from each of you and perfect my preparation process, which I am now able to share in this guide book, as a result of my 15 years devoted to all of you. Many of you have become dear friends and I hope you will credit yourself with the help this book provides to others that will embark on the divorce process.

Table of Contents

PREFACE

I like when I have options. We all do. When you are thinking about getting a divorce or have been served with divorce papers, it can often feel as if you are out of options. However, you do have options.

Your first option is to rush to an attorney, hire the first one you meet, are referred to, or the cheapest one you find, and immediately file for divorce. This option will then leave you with no strategic advantage, may leave you scrambling for funds for litigation, and worst of all will waste your money on unnecessary legal fees as your attorney is working with you to get all the information they require and putting out fires as a result of the rush. Some divorces can take two to three years due to one party being completely unorganized and unprepared for divorce.

Your second option is to follow this guide and prepare for a divorce. You will then be organized, knowledgeable, and prepared before even walking into an attorney's office. You will be armed with the power (as knowledge is power) to pick the appropriate attorney for you. You will save thousands of dollars in legal fees because you will have performed the upfront leg work so your attorney will not have to. This preparation, also makes it possible for your attorney to come up with the appropriate strategy for your case right at the

1

beginning, thereby giving you the ultimate advantage over the outcome of your divorce matter.

Studies show that we are more likely to act if we understand why it is important to do so. This guide will explain why it is imperative to prepare for a divorce in order to save time and money, decrease stress throughout the divorce process, and gain an advantage at the outset of your case. I will also provide you with a detailed road map, helping you prepare for divorce in a very systematic way.

It might seem that this book is only for initiators of divorce. However, the advice and guidance contained herein is just as important to follow for those who were blindsided by divorce. They should still go through the steps outlined in this guide to get through the divorce process and obtain the best possible outcome as a result of the divorce. Actually, if you are reading this because you just learned your spouse has filed or will be filing for divorce, I would start with Step 2: Gain Access to Funds, move on to Step 3: Build a Support Team, proceed to Step 1: Get Organized and then proceed to Step 4: Form the Proper Mindset. In fact, I would argue that forming a proper mindset, the last step of my step-by-step divorce preparation guide, is most crucial to those who have been blindsided by divorce, those who were just served with papers they never saw coming, or whose spouse simply got up and moved out of the family home in anticipation of divorce.

I hope whether you are the initiator or the one being divorced, you will read this guide, and keep referring to it on your path to a new beginning post-divorce.

"NOTHING SAYS A GOOD DAY LIKE A DIVORCE!" – IF YOU PREPARE FOR IT!

Before we start, I just want to mention those individuals who you and I should thank for making this guide book possible. I would like to thank, first and foremost, my husband, Ilan, for his patience, constant support, and unsolicited and solicited advice; my two boys, S & N, for providing me with cuddles, laughs, and distractions when I needed it most during the writing process; my assistant Amy Griffith for reading the manuscript, giving me great feedback, and for all her hard work running my law office and handling my day to day tasks, ultimately allowing me time to write and get this book completed; my editor, Russel Womack, for his professionalism, skill, feedback, responsiveness, and for taking a true interest in my work; my cover designer, Noel Sellon, for taking my embarrassing designs and turning them into "gold" – literally!; my muse, one of my closest friends and trusted advisor, Dalia Lightman, founder of Story of Life Therapy and Story of Life Photography, for taking the photo of me that graces the cover of this book, for your friendship, for allowing me to sit on your couch whenever necessary (both literally and figuratively), and for reviewing this guide and, as always, giving me honest and thoughtful feedback; my friend and amazing photographer, Jean Terman, founder of Jean Terman Photography, for taking my professional headshot used in the book and, by doing so, empowering me every time I look at it. Also, I can't forget the ladies who provided me with advice upon demand, Dominique Lauten and Allison Mentzel. Dominique, I must also thank you for reading the entire guide and providing me with your edits and hilarious commentary!

Last, but not least, I must thank all of my clients that I have had the privilege to represent. I have been able to learn from each of you and perfect my preparation process, which I am now able to share in this guide book, as a result of my 15 years devoted to all of you. Many of you have become dear friends and I hope you will credit yourself with the help this book provides to others that will embark on the divorce process.

INTRODUCTION

If you are reading this, you have triumphantly decided to change your life, protect your future, and properly prepare for a divorce. Let me assure you, the steps outlined in this guide will save you time and money; but most importantly, it will save you from sprouting many gray hairs as a result of the divorce process.

You may be thinking, *Helen Dukhan is a divorce attorney, so why would she go against herself and give me advice on how to save time and money during the divorce process?* If I had a nickel for every time I heard someone blame divorce attorneys for breaking up families to line their own pockets I would be a millionaire. However, that is just not the way I operate. I chose the practice of Divorce and Family Law because I felt it was the only area of law where I could make a difference. I get to ensure that my clients, their children, their financial future, their work and well-being are protected. I thought, *what is more important than "Family"?* Therefore, my goal was to do everything in my power to maintain "Family", despite divorce, rather than tear it apart. In fact, while I have never shied away from litigation, and, as my clients will tell you, I can be fierce when fighting to protect my clients' rights and their future, about 90% of my cases settle with the parties able to work as a family unit long after the divorce papers are signed and sealed. I often explain that I

5

believe that practicing divorce and family law is really one of the only things I truly excel at. Maybe it is because my clients can sense that I sincerely care about them rather than just making a buck.

One client who put his full trust in me, valued my level of experience, and heeded my advice throughout the entire divorce process, wrote me an email which said, "I followed your advice and proactively talked to her [his spouse]. With the help of one of our trusted friends, we actually resolved most of the differences between us and came to an agreement of how we were going to proceed in front of the mediator. We both hope for a peaceful resolution and to continue treating each other like close friends and family in the future." This client took my advice and spoke to his wife in order to try and resolve issues amicably between themselves and without wasting more money on counsel fees. His words solidify to me why I chose to practice family law in the first place and why I truly love what I do. In fact, my only goal is that instead of my clients being financially wiped out, emotionally destroyed, and forever bitter individuals, they are celebrating and proclaiming, "Nothing Says a Good Day Like a Divorce!"

"NOTHING SAYS A GOOD DAY LIKE A DIVORCE!" has been my motto since I found myself practicing Divorce and Family Law. I have it on magnets and say this to just about anyone who will listen. I should probably explain something since you are probably thinking this quack goes around suggesting that everyone should get divorced. I am not against marriage. In fact, I am married and have been for quite a long time. Actually, I am happy in my marriage (well, on most days). However, that being said, I do appreciate that sometimes in life things do not turn out as planned.

Marriage is hard and may sometimes feel unnatural, which can be exacerbated by the fact that we signed a legal contract to enter into it. Therefore, by getting a divorce you are breaking a legal contract, which seems crazy, since how can you base a legal contract on a person's feelings toward another person, which can change and fade? As with any other type of relationship, in most similar situations we are freely allowed to fix our mistakes, change our minds, and in fact are encouraged to "start over". But, for some odd reason, when a person gets married that is not the case. We discuss divorce as if it something to be ashamed of. People tend to feel sorry for those around them for going through or getting a divorce. The legal system has made it extremely costly, lengthy, and difficult to get a divorce. We hear horror stories of divorce all the time. Most of my clients still feel they cannot open up to family or friends about going through divorce so as not to be judged or ostracized, instead choosing to speak to a therapist or some other professional about what they are going through. They often choose Helen Dukhan Family Law to represent them because of our strong belief that we all make mistakes and should not be trapped in loveless and unhappy marriages, doomed to dealing with that decision for the rest of our lives. In fact, statistically speaking, 51% of all marriages end up in divorce.

That is where my motto, "Nothing Says a Good Day Like A Divorce" comes in. Often when I tell people my motto, they laugh thinking I am just being funny, that it's one of those lawyer jokes, or think it is a sad proclamation. I want to be clear that my motto is neither sad nor a laughing matter.

There is still a lot of stigma and shame surrounding divorce, and that is wrong. It's like any other choice in life you make — if you made a mistake, you are allowed to change your mind and celebrate your new beginning! There is enough negativity in this world without worrying about the negativity associated with divorce. Therefore, your goal should be that at the end of the divorce process you are jumping up and down like Tom Cruise on that infamous couch on Oprah (or on whatever you choose) screaming, "Nothing Says a Good Day Like A Divorce!"

However. There is always a BUT, right? To get to that place you must prepare. The divorce process, or any family court process, as a legal process, is hard. There is no sugar coating it. People often get frustrated by what seems like a vast sea between their notion of fairness and the court's definition of "equity". While neither I, nor any other attorney and/or professional regardless of their experience, length of time practicing, or any of their other stunning qualifications can predict the outcome of your divorce and/or give you that miracle magic way to get 100% of what you want and/or desire in your divorce, what I can give you is the gift of a process of preparation and gaining invaluable knowledge.

I hope to empower you to proceed with confidence so that you too can say, "Nothing Says a Good Day Like a Divorce!"

Helen M. Dukhan, Esq., LL.M

WHY PREPERATION FOR DIVORCE IS KEY!

I have dedicated the last fifteen years solely to the practice of divorce and family law, representing countless numbers of men and women in both New Jersey and New York. Over the years, it has become apparent to me that the most common misconception about divorce is that you can jump right into it without the proper planning and preparation. It is often said that we "fall" into love. Unfortunately, we should not make the same mistake and "fall" into divorce.

I can't tell you how many individuals come into my office demanding that I file their divorce documents — yesterday! However, if there is no emergency, threat to your well-being, or that of your children, following the consultation I almost always explain that if you want to be successful in your divorce and get the best possible outcome, you have to do a bit of preparing first (well, maybe a bit more than a bit).

I am fully aware that our modernized psyches are programmed for instant gratification, which leads many to foolishly believe that they will do just fine simply running into court and demanding a divorce. I mean, they know that their spouse is a lying, cheating, no good [whatever expletive you wish to insert here], and that any decent judge will agree and undoubtedly punish their spouse for all the bad things they have done, right? No — wrong! Most of the time it does not work that way.

In reality, if you fail to prepare, you will be disorganized, unaware of what to expect, scrambling to provide detailed information and documentation on last minute notice, and completely dependent on your attorney, the court, and outside experts to make key decisions about your life, your family, and your future, all while you are in the dark! You may be thinking that if it were necessary to prepare, then any qualified attorney would advise you to do the same. BUT, and this is a big BUT, your lack of preparation is wonderful for a divorce attorney since most bill by the hour, and your failure to prepare and get organized will enable the attorney to bill you for all of the time and extra effort that was expended organizing you. In fact, the attorney will have to clean up needless mistakes and oversights caused by lack of proof, documentation, and proper information. The icing on the cake is that they will be able to blame you for not being able to timely provide them with all the documentation and detailed information they require.

These pitfalls often lead to conflict between the unprepared and unaware client and the attorney, causing many to jump from one attorney to the next because they feel cheated and pressured to make certain decisions under time constraints and deadlines imposed by the courts. Often, those same individuals have no idea what the process might cost them, and due to their lack of preparation and their attorney billing to organize them, they run out of money for continued representation and litigation expenses early on at the outset of their case.

During a marriage you usually accumulate property, you accumulate money, you may have had children, you have your own interests, and you cannot simply fail to plan for divorce. If you do not take my word for it, maybe you would take the word of Benjamin Franklin who said the famous quote, "If you fail to plan, you plan to fail!" This applies to everything you do in life. If you have a business, you make a business plan; if you have children, you do your best to plan for their future and for college; if you are taking a vacation or traveling for business, you plan every detail. Getting divorced is no different.

Approximately 75% of the individuals I meet with during consultations -- or as I refer to them, education and strategy session -- believe that if their spouse makes a lot of money then it is guaranteed that the court will automatically grant them counsel fees and support right up front. They convince themselves that they will be able to afford to hit the ground running, which can cause them to spend all their money upfront, prior to even reaching the most complicated parts of the divorce process. This is the worst kind of misconception, because more often than not, if you have not planned in advance, if you are not aware of your finances, if you do not have the requisite proof and have not put yourself in a position to obtain such support, a judge will not award such support to you until the end of litigation or until you can prove your need for it. As a result, it can take months or even years for you to get the requisite funds you imagined you would easily get from your spouse, in effect putting you at a real disadvantage that could have easily been avoided with proper planning.

Those who are impatient and decide to shop around for an attorney who will quickly run them into court often come back to me to fix the mess that the other attorney made. They tell me that the other attorney made them big promises, guaranteed success, and charged them upwards of $20,000 during the first few months with little results. Sadly, this happens all too often.

Bottom line, divorces should be carefully planned for. Most people do not realize how much stress and needless litigation they can avoid and how much money they can save if they simply prepare themselves for divorce both financially and emotionally.

Let me give you an example. I had a client who came to me after more than twenty years in a terribly-unhappy marriage which she stayed in for the sake of her children. However, when the breakdown of the marriage was causing a nightmare situation for her and her children, she knew it was time to get divorced. She was a stay-at-home mother, had been out of the workforce for over 15 years, and had to prepare for life as a single parent with three children between the ages of 14 and 17. When she came to my office she had no money, no independent bank account, was emotionally run down, and had no idea how to get herself and her children out of the mess she was in. At our first meeting, she hired me to help her prepare for divorce. We discussed her goals, I managed expectations, and she left with a master plan in place to complete over the next three months. For the first time in twenty years, she was cruising down the road to freedom by following my GPS directions toward protecting her future and her children's well-being. After approximately three months we met again, discussed how far she had traveled, and began the next phase of her route. Prior to filing, we had to put her in a financial position to move her and her children out of the marital home, where the situation had become unbearable for all of them, to pay for legal fees, unexpected and expected expenses that might pop up as a result of litigation, and create a support network she could rely on during the process. Let me tell you, it was remarkable to see her go from a run down, emotionally exhausted, dependent wife, to a confident woman and independent lady boss. At the end of those three months, she found a home to rent in the same town, renewed her professional licenses, made enough money by doing a hobby she enjoyed doing, and with some help from her support network, she moved herself and her children out of the marital home.

With some creative planning and preparation, we were able to file an emergency application with the court for child support, litigation fees, and spousal support on the same day she moved out of her home, all of which were granted because of the yellow brick road we were able to pave during those short six months. In fact, not only was she awarded the monetary support she required right away, the success empowered my client, took loads of stress off her shoulders, and most importantly, put us at an advantage throughout the entire divorce process. In the end, we were able to avoid trial, as at least 80% of my cases do, by reaching a settlement agreement which ensured that my client was able to support herself, her children, their college education, and ensured that my client was awarded all that she was entitled to, which is always the ultimate goal.

As with so many of my clients who took the time and effort to plan and prepare for divorce, we now meet each year on my client's divorce-anniversary to celebrate their "Nothing Says a Good Day Like a Divorce!"

By exercising a bit of patience and heeding my advice and step-by-step directions and guidance through the divorce planning process you too can be on your road to happiness. However, every family dynamic and individual's circumstances are different and unique. Therefore, this guide is generalized to help you start on your road to exclaiming, "Nothing Says a Good Day Like a Divorce!" No information contained herein should be understood as legal advice or create an attorney/client relationship. Please understand, a competent and experienced divorce attorney should further tailor the information contained in this guide to your needs and situation.

Helen M. Dukhan, Esq., LL.M

HOW LONG SHOULD PREPARATION TAKE?

Many clients who are biting at the bit to move on and get divorced often wonder how long preparation should take. They did not want to prepare in the first place, and "patience is a virtue" that many do not want to practice. However, I urge you to realize that preparation is key and a must in order to save yourself from unnecessary stress and save you time and money.

The time period you must dedicate toward preparation for the divorce process is unique to each individual. For example, some people come in with their financial documents and details organized for me because they were the person in control of that area of their life, and they have funds to pay for divorce. Inevitably, there are always additional documents and information the attorney will request, but this individual will cruise through finalizing step one, skip step 2 because they already have sufficient funds to proceed, and all they will be left to accomplish is form the proper support team and proper mindset. How long it takes them to accomplish those steps really depends on them. The initiator of the divorce often believes that they can skip those steps because they are already in a good place emotionally and have the right people in their lives to help them achieve a positive outcome. However, I cannot stress

19

enough that every part of my preparation system is key to making the proper, non-emotional decisions toward a favorable outcome of the divorce process.

Every person's preparation time period is different, only you know if there are pressing issues or emergencies that require immediate attention. That being said, I would suggest that you give yourself at least three to six months (if you have that amount of time) for the preparation process as outlined in this book. I intentionally made this guide short, organized, and easy to digest so that it is a quick read allowing you to immediately start plowing through the steps.

Ultimately, *you* are the boss. Each of my clients is the boss of their case. I do not make them do anything. I definitely do not make them prepare if they are against doing so. However, I can assure you that after 15 years devoted solely to the field of family and divorce law, I can confidently state that those who took time preparing themselves for divorce and heeded my advice fared much better during and after divorce than those who did not.

WHAT IF YOU HAVE BEEN BLINDSIDED BY DIVORCE?

As previously mentioned, using this guide and following the steps provided are just as important and crucial to those who have been surprised by divorce. While your timeline may be different and somewhat abbreviated, it is still imperative for you to go through the steps outlined in this guide.

In whatever state you may be reading this from, once the initial divorce documents have been filed, they must be served upon the other spouse. Let's assume worst case scenario: you have been served with divorce documents you never saw coming. You will have a certain amount of days to respond, or as is often referred to as "Answer". Each state has different deadlines by which documents must be filed. Typically, in most states, I believe the served spouse has 30 – 35 days to Answer. This is definitely something you should discuss with an attorney. Keep in mind, depending on your state's deadline, you have that time frame to get some, if not all, of the steps contained in this guide completed or well on their way to being completed.

Immediately skip to Step 2 of this book, "Gain Access to Funds". Read Step 2 in its entirety. Then, stop, and figure out a way to quickly get access to as much of that goal amount as possible. You will need this to move on to Step 3, "Form Your Support Team". Once you have completed Step 2, move on to read Step 3 in its entirety. After reading about how to form a support team, stop before you go any further and do so! If you take my advice on the three essential team members who I believe every individual requires, you will be in the best possible position to proceed. Thereafter, with the help of your counsel and your support team, you can get through Step 1 and Step 4.

So, you may be thinking, *how will this guide save me money if I first have to hire an attorney?* The reality is, this book will save you time and money because you will know what to look for when hiring an attorney. You will walk into the attorney's office armed with confidence and knowledge, giving you the ability to make informed decisions. Then, after hiring your attorney, instead of bombarding your counsel with needless questions that the attorney will bill you for reading and answering, you will know exactly what your job is and what you have to do. By reading Step 1, "Get Organized", you know to ask for the Statement of Net Worth upfront so you can start filling it out. You know that while your attorney is working on an "answer" to their documents on your behalf, you should be getting organized and preparing the proper mindset. You are operating with knowledge, know-how and confidence. You will be able to form a big picture outlook which is future driven and cooperate with your attorney calmly and without having to put out fires at the last minute. You will be so busy working on yourself pursuant to the advice in this book that you will not be calling your attorney multiple times a day with questions and concerns, but instead allow your attorney to do their job and represent you diligently.

So, you see, even if you are the spouse surprised by the divorce, this book will still provide you with knowledge, which translates to power, and an easy step-by-step guide for preparing for, and getting through, the divorce process!

Helen M. Dukhan, Esq., LL.M

PREPARING FOR DIVORCE

There are four major steps to preparing for divorce. The steps are as follows: 1) Get Organized, 2) Gain Access to Funds, 3) Form a Support Team, 4) Develop Proper Mindset.

Each step is just as crucial and important as the others!

If you can, it is essential for success to take them step-by-step in the order that they are described. If you have already been served with divorce documents or do not feel as though you have the time to prepare as outlined in this book, please follow the directions in the previous section, "What If You Have Been Blindsided By Divorce".

You will find pages for notes as you go through this book. This is a guide which will provide you with a lot of information and give you work to do. In order to stay on track: be an active reader, take notes, make to-do lists as you read, and jot down thoughts and questions on the note pages provided. Even though I did not intend for this book to be a workbook, I included pages for notes so that you will be able to quickly refer to those notes if necessary, rather than having to re-read entire sections.

OK, are you ready? Let's get started!

Helen M. Dukhan, Esq., LL.M

CHAPTER 1

Step 1: Get Organized

While each step is crucial and just as important as the other, the extent to which you are able to get organized will determine how much upfront time and money you will save at the outset and during the divorce process. This step can be broken up into three parts: A) Gather Documentation & Information, B) Form a Budget, C) Start & Maintain a Journal.

Gather Information & Documentation:

Your first order of business in preparing for divorce is gathering as much information and documentation as possible. Here is a preliminary list of documents and information you should focus on obtaining.

- Bank Accounts: Checking/Savings
- Investment Accounts (stocks/bonds)
- Pension/Retirement Accounts (401K, IRA, pension)
- Credit Card Accounts (charge accounts)
- Pay stubs (keep most recent)
- W2s (prior year) or 1099s
- Tax Returns (including extension applications)
- Insurance Policies (health, home, auto)

- Loans (vehicle, personal, business, home equity, other)
- Real Property (mortgages, deeds, contracts, rental agreements, leases)
- Business (operation records, receipts, books)

This list is not exhaustive. If you come across any information and documentation that is not included on this list that you think your attorney should be aware of, include it.

Knowledge is power! While all documents can be subpoenaed and obtained during what is referred to as the discovery process of your divorce, it will save you much time and energy if you simply compile as much information and documentation as possible in advance. Any documents you can compile you should make a copy of and preferably organize in folders or binders to give to your attorney. The process of looking for and hiring an attorney will be discussed in Step 3: Forming a Support Team.

With all that being said, PLEASE PLEASE PLEASE do not do anything that will endanger your well-being or draw attention to your actions. Do not put yourself in danger by snooping around. I often advise my clients to be vigilant of documents that are lying around the house, but do not start opening mail you never opened before, or asking questions about finances you never previously inquired about. Rather, you could simply snap a picture of any envelope that comes home from any bank, financial institution, insurance company, or any other business that seems like a formal piece of mail and not junk mail. When in doubt, check it out! Later during the discovery process, your attorney will be able to ask your spouse specific questions about whether any assets or funds are held by certain institutions, or if the spouse has any affiliation with that business. Also, your attorney may make formal requests for documentation. If your spouse denies having any affiliation with an institution you believe they have dealings with, if you choose to do so, your attorney may subpoena records from that institution. If your spouse has funds or assets there, the institution, pursuant to the Subpoena, will have to provide you with records proving so.

Many individuals come in to my office and explain that their spouse handles all the finances and that they have no access to any information. They are often surprised to hear that they are easily able to get their hands on much more crucial information than they realize. Reality is, the one document that provides the most detailed information and is the easiest to obtain are your tax returns. In order to obtain a copy of your tax return, you can request one from the IRS by going to their website. As long as your name and social security number appear on the tax return, you will be able to obtain a copy of the return and any documents attached to it.

29

Do not panic if you are thinking, *the tax returns are not accurate because you are absolutely sure your crooked spouse's accountant failed to include all income or claimed thousands in false deductions.* This is often the case where one spouse owns their own business and other similar circumstances. However, while certain figures may not be correct, which your attorney can advise you how to deal with, the tax return still contains important information that your attorney must know about. Your tax returns will provide you with a wealth of information, including bank account information, interest information, rental income, any properties you may not be aware of, any pension or retirement accounts, stocks, other investments, etc. This is arguably the most important document for you to obtain and provide to your attorney. In most cases, with the tax return in hand, I can provide my clients with very accurate estimations of how much support they will be able to receive, form a budget for them, and provide other important strategies and options regarding their financial well-being.

It is the worst when a client comes in and states that they have no access to the tax return, that their husband has it, or the accountant has it and we get served with divorce paperwork without ever having seen a copy of the tax document. Lack of information can be crippling to your ultimate success in the divorce process.

Therefore, before anything else, you should work as diligently as possible to obtain as much information and documentation as possible before moving on to the next step.

Furthermore, running a credit report could provide you with important details of your accounts, credit cards, and important bank information you may have overlooked, forgotten about, or simply been unaware of. Countless times clients realize that their spouse, without their consent or knowledge, opened an account in their name that was ruining their credit. While you may be blindsided by divorce, you definitely do not want to be blindsided by something that can have a lasting impact on your financial health. Your attorney should be able to help you deal with such issues.

NOTES:

_____

_____

_____

_____

_____

_____

_____

_____

_____

Form a Budget:

In most states, you will have to fill out a very detailed Statement of Net Worth, which details all your income, expenses, assets, and liabilities. In New Jersey, it is called a Case Information Statement. Each state refers to this document differently, but they all request approximately the same information. The form is generally a sworn document and is arguably the most important document you will file during your divorce process and should be completed with the guidance and assistance of an experienced divorce attorney. However, to get you organized, you should obtain this document and start filling it out immediately. You may be able to download the required form online. If you cannot get the required document online, you should download one of many available programs or apps for creating a detailed budget. In order to properly fill out this document or prepare to do so, you should start to collect your receipts, and begin to really monitor your spending, fixed expenses, and debts. You can request credit card statements, bank account statements, or any other statements you need in order to figure out how much you spend each week, each month, each quarter, each six-month period, and during the year.

It is a very good idea to break down the income, expenses, and debts of the family into three categories: 1) family, 2) children, and 3) individual. The numbers you obtain should not be guesses. Not even educated or informed guesses! Rather, the final figures should be as accurate as possible. This will give you and your attorney the proper information to create a budget to ensure that you are able to support yourself, your children, and ensure your financial stability post-divorce. It is important for the Court to maintain your standard of living to the extent possible. Divorce is all about planning for the future, and forming a proper budget is the key to doing so.

If you have children, you should start to compile a list of their activities, including extracurricular activities, school activities, play dates, memberships, etc. You should start to print out or catalogue any fixed expenses related to the children, and any additional expenses that pop up. If the children attend private school, you should obtain a record of how many years they have been enrolled in the private school, tuition for each year that has been paid, copies of any checks that have been written to the private school or credit card statements of payments made to the school. You should request a breakdown of all monthly and yearly expenses related to the school and provide proof of whether you, your spouse, or you both pay the expenses.

It is important to provide documentation of medical bills, dental bills, bills from mental health providers, bills from therapy if your children see a therapist, or any other necessary medical, dental, or therapeutic expenses your children require.

Also, do not forget to include the mortgage, home owner's insurance, costs that you spend on average for upkeep of the home, repairs, and any other necessary expenses relating to the home, and any other properties you own. This also applies to any businesses you or your spouse may own or have any interest in, and any loans, debts, and liabilities you may have whether in your name or your spouse's name.

In most cases depending on your financial circumstances, except where one spouse is considered to be in the extremely high net worth category, the spouse will have to calculate how much they will need to earn to save sufficiently for divorce, and how much they will require to maintain a comparable standard of living following the marriage to that which they enjoyed during the marriage. Due to the income of the spouse, one will often have to figure out the standard they are able to settle for. Many times, following the preparation of the budget, the spouse who wishes to stay in the marital residence realizes they are unable to afford to do so and would be better off having the house sold or being bought out of their interest by the other spouse. Forming a budget and knowing what you require to secure your financial future, such as whether you will need funds to re-enter the work force or obtain further education, is crucial to proper preparation and success during your divorce. You may need to meet with a financial advisor or accountant for help to educate you regarding your options and consequences of each option. Keep in mind; a budget is absolutely necessary to recognize if you can afford any such experts to help you during the divorce process.

Finally, regarding this step, I must note that forming a proper, supported, and well thought out budget and financial picture for you and your family is most important if you plan on moving out of the marital residence, especially if you are planning to move out with your children. My rule of thumb is you must make sure that you have enough to support you and the children, and pay for the costs of litigation, for at least six months. Having a detailed and properly thought out budget will help you plan accordingly.

Let me assure you, that while this may all seem very daunting and just reading this may be sending you into a tailspin, you are not alone. I have had clients that have hardly any information, very limited means, no accounts, no credit cards of their own and little financial knowledge learn how to attain their financial goals, be able to fund their divorce, and obtain the support they need both during

and after divorce. They were able to do so, by setting realistic goals

based upon an accurate budget.

NOTES:

_____

_____

_____

_____

_____

_____

_____

_____

_____

_____

_____

_____

_____

_____

_____

_____

_____

_____

_____

Helen M. Dukhan, Esq., LL.M

Start & Maintain a Journal:

I must first explain what I mean by a journal, because I do not mean a locked diary with lined sheets. In my mind I envision a folder. In that folder I would have lined sheets for writing on, a calendar and pockets for paper work. I should probably call this journal a binder of sorts that you create for yourself.

On the lined sheets of paper, you should maintain a journal wherein you write your goals, your concerns, and daily thoughts. This will be a safe place for you to jot down any phone numbers, addresses, bank account numbers, or additional information that is important to you. Also, you should be documenting any information you wish to tell your attorney, including any concerns, fears, and questions. More often than not, I tell my clients not to discuss their issues with friends or family who have been through divorce as each family is unique, the outcomes may be very different, and the advice they receive or stories they hear could seriously make their head spin. However, it is important for you to do some research at least with regard to the laws in your state and questions you should ask an attorney at a consultation.

Note any questions that apply to your situation down in your journal. Inevitably, the first meeting with any attorney is an experience you have probably never been through and never contemplated going through. If you are not organized and prepared, you may leave the initial consultation just as lost and in the dark regarding your options as when you first walked in. More about finding the right attorney will be discussed in Step 3.

In your journal, decide what you want from your divorce. Before you research any information about how much support you may be entitled to, who gets to keep what piece of furniture or the family pet, think in generalities and consider the big picture. Focus on what you want your future to look like post-divorce and jot down your ideal situation. Keep these issues in mind:

1. Alimony/Spousal Support
2. Division of Real Property (house, building, land)
3. Division of Debts
4. Insurance Policies and Premiums
5. Child Support
6. Custody (decision making, physical custody, visitation)
7. Division of Personal Property (furniture, cars, appliances, etc)
8. Changing Back to your Maiden Name
9. Bank Accounts
10. Pension/Retirement Accounts/Brokerage Accounts

In your journal, also consider how you want the divorce process to go. Do you think you are a good candidate for mediation, a neutral third party to help you and your spouse to come to an amicable agreement? Do you think that your spouse will put up a fight about certain aspects of your divorce? Do you think that you may have to file an emergency request for fees or support to the court? What is your ideal situation as to how the divorce process will progress? You will discuss this with your attorney who will help you with the pros and cons of each of your wishes and the cost of each option.

Your journal should also contain an inventory of your personal property. In most cases the marital home is sold, and proceeds split according to an agreement or a court order. In some circumstances one spouse can stay in the marital home, maybe for the stability of the children, or if the house is separate property (any property purchased by one spouse prior to the marriage). Either way, you should start to consider which pieces of personal property (furniture, appliances, etc.) you wish to keep and make list in your journal to discuss with your attorney. Some manuals, guides and blogs will encourage you to start taking such belongings out of the home and storing them at secret places. I do not agree with this advice in most circumstances because the Courts frown upon such

41

actions and may even punish a spouse for taking such actions. I did state that I do not believe such actions should be taken in "most circumstances" because I believe there are sometimes exceptions. In cases where you have a family heirloom that you truly cannot live without, jewelry that you believe is your separate property, photo albums that you made and mean the world to you, and other such small mementos that you absolutely cannot live without, believe you have the right to, and do not want to take the risk of them disappearing or getting destroyed, then I let my client know they can remove those items from the home and keep them somewhere safe until it is finally decided upon who gets those items.

Your journal, or binder, should also contain a calendar for record keeping. This will allow you to keep track of dates and deadlines that your attorney informs you of. Yes, an old school calendar written in with a pen of any color you choose. I do not trust technology and think that anything encompassed on your computer or phone can be tracked and broken into and I always recommend keeping everything private and in writing.

Lastly, regarding this step, your journal should have pockets and possible additional folders inside of it for record keeping. Before long, you will be drowning in a sea of paperwork. You will want to organize your documents that you obtain for your lawyer, documents you receive from your lawyer, documents you receive from the court, and documents you receive from professionals or experts assisting you with your case, etc.

The bottom line is that the more organized you are with your documents, time, thoughts and concerns, the less stress you will experience and the more time and money you will save.

NOTES:

_____

_____

_____

_____

_____

_____

_____

_____

_____

_____

_____

_____

_____

_____

_____

CHAPTER 2

Step 2: Gain Access to Funds

I am often asked how much a divorce typically costs. This is impossible to answer as so many factors are out of my control. As with most questions you might ask during your divorce process, the answer to this question is always, "It depends". However, I always recommend that prior to filing for a divorce you have at least $10,000 saved. That means that the golden rule is that you should have $10,000 in disposable cash in a bank account prior to filing for divorce.

You may be thinking there is absolutely no way you would ever be able to get access to or earn $10,000. However, I believe that where there is a will, there is a way. Many of my clients are stay at home parents, their spouse does not make enough to pay for their legal expenses, and they need to move out of their home, must support their children, and due to their sheer determination to attain happiness and freedom find a way to fund their divorce and life during the process.

I want to be clear that I am not recommending leaving your marital residence or removing your kids from the marital residence. In fact, for the most part, I always recommend, if possible, staying in the marital home until either of two things happens: 1) you and your spouse come to an agreement as to the disposition of the marital home, or 2) until a court decides how the home will be disposed of. However, the reality of it is that in some circumstances the client simply must move out of the home and sometimes needs to remove the children from the home. Either way, you will need to obtain funds for whatever course you decide you must take.

You always have options, such as:

- Borrow money from family and/or friends
- Apply for and obtain a credit card
- Take half of any joint bank account
- Obtain a loan from the bank
- Take a loan from your pension or retirement account
- Get a second job (some turn hobbies into extra cash, i.e., photography)
- Put away certain amounts of cash into a separate account over a prolonged period of time

I am sure that this list of options to save up enough money to start a divorce is not exhaustive of all options, but it should give you an idea of some options that might work for you.

You must also be aware that $10,000 may very well be the minimum amount you pay for a divorce, but you are likely to spend more in order to obtain an outcome you can live with. There is no way for an attorney to predict how much you will spend, but if you find the proper attorney, you should be kept apprised of your financial standing at each step of the divorce and educated as to all alternatives, options, and the cost of each so that you do not run out of money before obtaining that which you are entitled to during the divorce process. You should be extremely clear of your attorneys billing practices, how often you will get a billing statement, all fees that may not be included in your retainer fee, and all out-of-pocket costs you should expect for experts or other professionals the court may require.

That being said, depending on your financial circumstances, the judge may very well award you immediate child support, spousal support, and litigation fees. I always tell my clients that they should still have the requisite amount of money saved up just in case it does not go as planned, and for unexpected expenses that might pop up along the way. However, I also let them know my opinion based on years of experience whether I believe they have a chance of getting their legal fees covered, and to what extent. Your attorney should do the same by providing you with honest opinions of the possible and likely outcomes of your requests. They say you can't get blood from a stone and so is the case in divorce matters. If your spouse cannot afford to maintain two separate households and pay for your litigation fees at the same time as paying their own, the court will not put your spouse in an impossible situation of paying your fees. One must take a realistic look at the big picture devoid of emotions when thinking how the court will decide on certain aspects of the case.

First things first — before beginning your journey to gain access to funds, you must either open a separate bank account at an institution completely separate and apart from any your spouse banks with, or determine that your money will all be in cash and decide where you will keep the cash. I always recommend opening a separate bank account for funds you may need to receive during the divorce, and as a result of the divorce process, and thereafter. A third option is paying expenses by credit card. To do so you will have to apply for a credit card if you do not already have one of your own. If you are applying for a credit card, you should consider your credit and whether you can obtain one with no interest for 12-18 months. Therefore, you will only have to make minimal payments for quite some time without being charged interest and may not need a separate bank account right away. This is a great way to build your credit for the long run, as when you pay off the balance your credit score will increase significantly. Just be careful to check the fine print of any such credit card before signing up for one.

A few things you should be aware of: 1) if you take a loan from your pension or retirement account, you may suffer severe tax penalties and consequences. You should seek financial advice before doing so, 2) if you take money from your joint bank account, you should only take up to half. But that does not mean you are entitled to half; therefore, you may be forced by the court to pay some amount back to your spouse, 3) anything you earn during the preparation time and prior to filing for divorce is considered marital property which your spouse may have a claim to. The cutoff date regarding marital assets is the date you file for divorce. This means that anything earned or purchased after one spouse formally files for divorce is considered separate property. However, waiting three to six months to file for divorce in order to prepare for it sufficiently typically makes no significant difference in the amount of assets that will be considered marital, and therefore subject to distribution — unless, you win the lottery, of course!

Lastly, with regard to gaining access to funds, you may need to provide a mailing address to receive statements, bills, etc. For example, any credit card company will require a mailing address to send your card to. If you do not wish for your spouse to know about your actions prior to the divorce papers being served upon them, it is important for you to either open a P.O. Box for mail or provide the address of a trusted family member, friend, or business.

NOTES:

Nothing Says a Good Day Like a DIVORCE If You Prepare for it!

Helen M. Dukhan, Esq., LL.M

CHAPTER 3

Step 3: Form a Support Team

The next step is to form a support team. The reason I call it a "Support Team" is because I do not simply mean a support group or support system — I mean a "team" in every sense of the word. I want you to do some deep down soul searching and determine what kind of support you require. Here are some options:

1. Divorce/Family Law Attorney
2. Friends
3. Family
4. Social Worker
5. Therapist (psychiatrist, psychologist)
6. Financial Advisor/Planner
7. Accountant
8. Divorce Coach
9. Life Coach
10. Organizer
11. Personal Assistant
12. Babysitter, Au pair, Nanny, Mother's Helper
13. Cleaning Lady
14. Pastor, Priest, Rabbi, Spiritual Advisor

During a divorce, I find that most of my clients are in a funnel. I can imagine it is like being inside of a tornado, not that I have ever been in the eye of a tornado, but I imagine that most of my clients feel like they are trapped inside of one when going through divorce. A lot of the time, I realize that my clients are all consumed with the issues of the divorce because, well, let's face it, divorce affects each and every issue of life as we know it. Therefore, it is incredibly important to form a "Support Team" before entering the funnel.

Just consider the following: if you have children, you may need to be available for court, to meet with your attorney, to meet with an expert or evaluator upon last minute notice, and you may need help caring for your children during those times. Also, because you will quickly realize that the most well-meaning individuals can still be judgmental, incapable of giving an unbiased opinion and simply lending a listening ear, you might require a professional who will listen and help guide your emotions such as a psychologist. If you suffer from depression or anxiety, this is not the time to neglect your mental and emotional well-being. In fact, to the contrary, you may seek out a psychiatrist who can assist you in getting through it all. If you know that you and/or your spouse have pensions, retirement accounts, brokerage accounts, or other asset plans, you will need to understand those plans, understand the survivor benefits, understand their tax implications and transferability options, and possibly set up new accounts that will help you avoid some possible financial landmines you may not even know to consider. Therefore, you may require the assistance of an accountant or financial advisor. I am sure that you are able to understand by this point what I mean by Form a Support Team.

I often recommend having, at minimum, one best friend, a therapist, and a divorce/family law attorney as part of your support team. If you require any of the additional suggestions listed above, then the more the merrier as long as you keep the negativity out. I'm sure you have heard that famous African proverb, "It takes a village!" Well, it really does to get through a divorce.

I'm sure you are thinking, *of course a divorce attorney would list Divorce/Family Law Attorney first on their list of who should be a part of the Support Team.* However, let me assure you that I have a very valid reason for doing so. I cannot even begin to tell you how many men and women come into my office who have been given horrible advice by well-meaning or simply back-stabbing family members and friends. I mean, earth shattering bad advice, that if followed would have quite possibly destroyed any reasonable outcome that individual may have hoped for at the conclusion of their divorce. Yes, their advice was that bad!! Finding a divorce attorney to head your support team is a must! In fact, your divorce attorney may be the best referral source to you when building your support team as most divorce attorneys who specialize in the divorce field have their own support team of therapists, accountants, child custody evaluators, life coaches, divorce coaches, mediators, etc. These are professionals who have been vetted by your attorney and are money well spent since your attorney can probably vouch for the quality of their assistance.

Notice that I don't just list "Attorney" at the top of the list. I specify Divorce/Family Law Attorney since it is incredibly important to find an attorney who specializes in Divorce and Family Law. As some states do not allow their attorneys to state that they specialize in a certain field of law, you should hire that attorney whose sole focus has always been Family and Divorce Law. The worst mistake you can make is to retain a family friend who practices commercial litigation, but does an occasional divorce case, and represents you as a favor to you. The field of family law is a very specialized field with its own body of laws, a small and tight knit legal community, and case law that occasionally requires years of experience to understand and apply. Just as you would seek out a specialist to cure you from a rare disease, you need a specialist to cure you from, well....ok, you get the idea. Just as significant, a lawyer with years of experience in the field has inevitably been before the family law judges countless times or knows who has and can discuss that judge's expectations, rulings, and preferences with them. Having an attorney aware of the preferences of each judge, what drives them crazy, and how they usually rule on any given issue is invaluable. With this sort of knowledge comes the power of persuasion and is exactly what one must look for when hiring the right attorney.

There is no shame in consulting more than one attorney and I often advise that my clients do so. I think you need to really like your attorney in order to trust your attorney. You will be spending significant time either on the phone or in person working with your attorney. As much as you may think an attorney is experienced or knowledgeable, if you do not like them or their approach, you should not hire them.

I have some questions I think it is imperative you ask each attorney you consult with, which are as follows:

1. Do you specialize in divorce? How long have you been solely devoted to divorce and family law?

2. How long do you take to return phone calls? What happens if I need to reach you in case of emergency? Do you often check emails? How accessible are you?

3. Will any one else be working on my case? What experience do they have? Can I meet them?

4. What is your fee structure? How am I billed? What are the other costs I can expect?

5. What are my options? What do you believe is the best strategy for my case?

6. What is the percentage of cases you have that settle?

7. Have you represented any clients in divorce trials before?

As a solo practitioner, my clients know that they will only be working with me. They are assured that because of the small nature of my practice they will get my hands-on attention to their case every step of the way. I explain to my clients that they can call any time and I will call them back within 24 hours, but I am almost always available by email and they will get an occasional email from me at midnight or 6:00 AM. It is imperative to work with a family law attorney who truly cares that you are going through turmoil and may need them at last minute's notice and cannot wait days for a response. I think experience, a personal touch, and accessibility are the most important characteristics of any attorney that you should look for. Of course, you must be able to afford the attorney. Let me assure you an attorney's fees do not make them worthy of your business. However, an attorney who charges a very low fee as compared to other attorneys in the local community is probably desperate for business or is not as experienced as others. Lastly, I would recommend that you figure out if the attorney is extremely adversarial and argumentative, or values an amicable approach and has a high settlement rate. While I have faith in most members of my profession, there are too many divorce attorneys who tarnish the reputation of the rest by causing problems for the parties, the client, and everyone involved simply to bill more. Please be wary of those attorneys who want to get out of the gate running, promising to crush the other side, file motions for relief, and makes mountains out of molehills when it does not seem necessary. This is where you have to follow your gut and, if necessary, get a second, third or even fourth opinion.

How to find the right attorney to represent you in a divorce matter could be an entire book unto itself. For more tips and advice, you can check out my blog post that discusses a summary of my best advice for doing so at: https://hdfamilylaw.com/qualities-new-york-divorce-lawyer/

NOTES:

CHAPTER 4

IS AN ATTORNEY ABSOLUTELY NECESSARY?

I assume that if you are reading this guide you are either thinking of getting a divorce or were recently served with divorce documents. I am going to go one step further and assume that if you are reading this book, you believe you need to prepare for a divorce, so you do not think it will be an "easy" uncontested divorce. What I mean is that some clients call me and explain that both spouses have discussed getting a divorce, they may not have children or much property, or they already have a resolution to such issues and they simply want an attorney to draft the proper paperwork and get them a quick divorce. I refer to such divorces as uncontested divorces because the spouses are not contesting anything.

In the true uncontested divorce circumstance, I may answer the question of whether you absolutely need a divorce attorney as — it depends, but in any other circumstance where there are any contested issues, or outstanding issues that just may not be resolved easily, my answer would unequivocally be — ABSOLUTELY!

Here is an analogy that might help you decide. You wake up in the morning with the sniffles, a headache, aches and pains typical of a cold or flu. You go about your day and it progressively gets worse. You have been self-medicating, drinking lots of tea, and trying to get as much rest as possible to get rid of the bug you have. You think you should go see a doctor but decide why would I go and pay that steep co-pay when they will probably just tell me its viral and there is nothing they can do about it. A day later, WHAM! You wake up with a migraine, your head feels like it is going to explode, and you rush into your doctor only for them to diagnose you with a severe sinus infection, strep throat and an ear infection, that probably could have all been prevented if you had simply gone to see the doctor after the first couple of days when you noticed your sniffles were not going away.

Divorce should be treated similarly. If you know it's an uncontested divorce, with no issues to resolve or everything is already resolved, then you simply have the sniffles and they will go away without a specialist. However, you will have to go to court and spend time there in order to understand how to draft the vast amount of paperwork required to be filed in an uncontested divorce and learn about the procedure involved to finally get your divorce judgment signed. So, while you may not absolutely "need" an attorney, you may just find it easier to hire one to do the paperwork and legwork for you. On the other hand, if you know your divorce has outstanding issues that need to be resolved and you have no idea whether it is going to be a piece of cake or like having full on pneumonia trying to resolve them, or if you are certain you are one step away from the divorce ER, you absolutely need a divorce attorney to represent you.

If you decide not to retain a divorce attorney, or as the law refers to it, go *pro se*, please secure thousands of dollars more in funds as you will have to start ordering law books and manuals, and hiring experts and professionals to assist you. You will need to teach yourself the vast body of law, procedures, paper work, and court standards that control each and every divorce. You could go on line and try to find your answers on the legal equivalent to WebMD or you could seek out an attorney who will guide you through the process to cure what ails you.

Divorce is a tricky thing. You will not believe how much paperwork is involved to simply start the case. Then, if you have any issues to resolve, such as custody, parenting time, child support, alimony, or distribution of property, you have to know the case law, the statutory formulas, the statutory laws, and the court standards that govern such issues. Most attorneys who do not practice family law will usually avoid family law cases because of the complexities and the sheer amount of gray area that only attorneys who solely focus on divorce and family law would know how to deal with.

The Huffington Post lists 5 reasons why you should hire an attorney (https://www.huffpost.com/entry/5-reasons-that-you-need-a_b_3937368):

1) Expert Advice 2) Reduce Stress 3) Avoid Mistakes 4) Clear and Binding Agreements, and 5) Avoid Delays. Do you and your spouse really want to be yelling at each other over every little thing only to get to court and realize the demands you were both making are not even possible options according to the Court? Or, even worse, bring an agreement to the court after hours of diligently working to resolve your issues, only to realize you are missing key information or court language the court requires. The kicker is, if this happens, the judge is not permitted to give you any legal advice on how to fix it.

I am in no way saying that divorce without an attorney is impossible. However, I strongly do not recommend going at it alone and leaving your finances, property, and issues regarding your rights as a parent up in the air without the proper protection and representation. Your future depends on the outcome of your divorce; do not gamble on it to save a few bucks.

Having said that, please do not mistake hiring an attorney to represent you as hiring an attorney to make your decisions for you or operate without having to explain the process to you. Take an active part in your divorce. You will have to live with your decisions long after the divorce is finalized. Make sure you are aware of all your options, that your attorney communicates with your regularly, answers all your questions, and makes sure to fight for your goals. REMEMBER THIS — YOU ARE THE BOSS! The attorney is a consultant, counselor, and your representative. CEOs have people who recommend which actions they should take based on unique knowledge, education, and experience. You are the CEO of your life and your attorney is there to recommend which actions you should take, why you should take those actions, what they believe is possible, and how you can save yourself time, stress, and money, while achieving an acceptable outcome for you. I have heard of attorneys yelling at their clients, making them feel that they did not have a choice in their own future and family matters, or made the client feel guilty for going against their advice. That should never be the case. You should always be your own biggest advocate and make sure you and your attorney work as a team toward a common goal — securing your future, protecting your rights, and fighting for what you are entitled to.

NOTES:

_____

_____

_____

CHAPTER 5

Step 4: Form the Proper Mindset

Let me start this section by stating that I am not a psychologist and have no mental health training whatsoever. However, I have guided and counseled more clients over the years than I can count through the divorce process in both New York and New Jersey. Remember, I have only practiced divorce and family law during my legal career and have advance training in the field. Therefore, I have come to recognize a thing or two about the mindset you must have in order to get through your divorce process and move on from the divorce process.

This is what I mean by the proper mindset. I break this up into five categories: A) Financial Mindset, B) Self-Reflection, C) Acceptance, D) Gratitude, and E) Activity. I will go through each individually, but I must give you one piece of advice first. All of the categories that form a proper mindset should be addressed while you prepare for the divorce. You should allow yourself a chance to start working on each individually. However, personal growth does not happen over night, and I do not want you to believe I am suggesting you wait to file for divorce until you have completely arrived at the proper mindset. I am suggesting that you give it a good start. You should read through each category, process what each means, start to discuss them with your therapist if you chose to utilize one, and do the exercise I suggest you do. This, along with the previous steps, will help you immensely in starting the divorce off on the right foot. You will then carry the proper mindset with you throughout the divorce, build upon the progress you have made, continue with the exercises and activities, and ultimately get to a place where you can honestly say, "Nothing Says a Good Day Like a Divorce!" Ok, that being said, let's get to the categories that come together to form a proper mindset.

Financial Mindset:

Divorce can get very messy and very costly. Neither you nor your attorney may be able to control the cost of divorce if your spouse or your spouse's attorney is especially difficult. Therefore, before you go into a panic about your finances and the amount of debt you may have to accrue in order to survive during divorce and thereafter, break your mindset about finances into two boxes. In one box you have the cost of divorce and in the other you have the price of divorce.

The price of divorce is how much you actually pay. This is the hourly rate and the retainer you pay your attorney. This is the actual amount of money you have to pay to have your documents filed, hire experts to assist in the divorce, and any other expenses you may encounter along the way.

The cost of divorce is the effect you allow it to take on your life. The cost you will bear if you fail to pay a specialized attorney for their services and knowledge. The cost it will have on your life if you do not invest in the correct support team to help you through the divorce process and prepare for a life post-divorce.

You must decide how important it is for you to achieve certain goals during the divorce, i.e. support, custody, retirement, etc. Then you must decide the cost of failing to pay the price to achieve these goals.

I always sit down with each client before allowing them to take any actions or make any decisions, and I review the price versus the cost of each decision. I believe some in economic circles may refer to this as the cost-benefit analysis. However, I don't look at the cost as the price you will pay for that decision or action, I focus on the cost of it on your life, or your children's life if you do or don't.

Thereby, it is imperative for you to decide what it will cost you if you do not pay the price for proper representation, proper assistance, or any other financial investment you may have to make during the divorce process.

Also, on the topic of the proper financial mindset, it is extremely important to note that while you are making decisions based upon present circumstances, you MUST become a psychic who can foretell the future. Every decision you make must be based upon what your future needs and concerns will be. During the divorce process, the agreement or order will determine how you move on into the future. Again, going back to what this article is all about, "If you fail to plan, you are planning to fail!" – Benjamin Franklin. Therefore, do not fixate on the present, but look forward toward a bright and happy future of abundance, independence and new beginnings, and make sure you financially plan for that with every decision you make during the divorce process.

NOTES:

_____

_____

_____

_____

_____

_____

_____

_____

Self-Reflection:

When in a relationship and especially during marriage, it is very easy to lose track of who you are as a person, as an individual. We associate ourselves with being a spouse, a parent, a breadwinner or homemaker. In fact, every experience in our life makes us who we are at any given point in our lives. Some serious self-reflection will help you separate yourself from your role as a spouse and really help you gain independence as a person separate and apart from anything else.

When taking stock of who you are as an individual, you must go through challenges. This does not mean that you are going to throw yourself a pity party or wallow in your own self-criticism (for more than ten minutes). Rather, it means that you will take responsibility for any actions that may have led to the breakdown of your marriage. They say it takes two to tango. Well, it is often very difficult to go through a divorce with a victim mentality. When you can only see yourself as a victim, your demands may be clouded in emotion, anger, and resentment. However, the legal system does not operate on emotions and feelings — it operates on applying the laws to the facts of each case. Therefore, while your emotions will inevitably play some part in your decision making, by taking responsibility for your own actions, feelings, and thoughts, it often helps in realizing that maybe, just maybe, you just did not work together, and might make better people being apart. The goal is to really take account of your emotions, realize that you both need to take a certain amount of responsibility for your actions and feelings, and while that may not excuse certain behaviors in any way, it does tame decisions based purely on emotions.

That being said, if you are the victim of domestic abuse, have been cheated on, or are the victim of emotional abuse or have been living with a narcissist, I of course am not insinuating that you should take responsibility for any of those behaviors or for the divorce. However, in those cases you should take responsibility for the choice you made that enough is enough and choosing to get a divorce. Immediately after taking responsibility for this choice, I want you to feel strong and confident and pat yourself on the back, do a happy dance, or whatever other celebrating you can do, because you are one step closer to happiness and freedom. If you have heeded the advice in this guide, you also have gone through some deep self-reflection as to the person you are, independent of your role as a spouse, independent of the abuse, independent of your chains, and can breathe a sigh of relief that you get to be that wonderful person once again. You get a take two.

In fact, every person reading this book should begin to feel that inner confidence. You have decided that you require a new beginning, to grow as a person, to have a second chance. Take full responsibility for that feeling, because my friend, that is a bold and courageous move!

NOTES:

_____

_____

_____

_____

_____

_____

_____

_____

_____

_____

_____

_____

_____

_____

_____

Nothing Says a Good Day Like a DIVORCE If You Prepare for it!

Acceptance:

Ok, I'm going to give you exactly 10 minutes to grieve. Experts suggest that even if you are the initiator of the divorce, it is very important for you to grieve the loss of a marriage. Even if you are the initiator, you may be feeling pain, anger, fear, or guilt. Therefore, it is suggested that you grieve the loss of your marriage and process those emotions and feelings. Earlier in this guide I suggested that your support team must include a therapist. I believe that it is extremely helpful to my clients to process their emotions with the help of a professional that can guide them through all the highs and lows they may feel during the divorce. In fact, I come from a culture that does not really believe in therapy, so for me to be suggesting that you utilize a professional's help and expertise means that I have myself witnessed how much value it brings to my clients who choose to take my advice. However, for purposes of this section of the book, I believe that you must take a few minutes to grieve the end of the marriage in order to be able to delve into some deep self-reflection and uncover the person who you are. Get rid of the "If only this" and "If only that" feelings and simply have a funeral for the marriage. If you need to throw away photos, go for it; if you need to have a night out with friends and cry, go for it, anything you need to do — do it, as long as it is not dangerous or life threatening. As long as whatever you choose to do does not involve starting a bad habit or addiction, just get to a place that you ACCEPT IT so you can swiftly move on.

NOTES:

_____

_____

_____

_____

_____

_____

_____

_____

_____

_____

_____

_____

_____

_____

_____

_____

_____

Gratitude:

I give most of my clients an exercise to do at the very outset of the divorce process, or at the beginning of wherever they are on their road to divorce. I tell them to sit down with their journal and list all the negative emotions, feelings, and thoughts they have toward their spouse, their divorce, and their life at that moment. Then, I ask them to flip every one of the negative aspects they have written down around into a positive statement. Once they are done with that exercise, I ask them to list everything they are grateful for based on that list and to add anything else they might be grateful for separate and apart from their marriage, their spouse, and their role in their current life.

I ask you to do the same thing. The more you can do to feel grateful, the better the outcome of the divorce will be. The more you are able to let go of certain negative emotions, the more logical your decisions will be and the more money you will save bargaining for the things you truly need, rather than those with sentimental value. Gratefulness helps you think in terms of the big picture, which inevitably helps you think in the long run and separate yourself from the here and now. This ability is crucial to experiencing lower stress, saving time and money, and achieving the best possible outcome.

Since the divorce process ebbs and flows, sometimes feeling like a roller coaster of epic proportions, I recommend that you re-read these lists, add to them daily, and to really allow yourself to feel grateful for those things on the list despite anything else that might be going on in your life at that moment. It will not only greatly help you in preparing for divorce, but it will help you finish the process with acceptance, gratefulness, and dignity.

NOTES:

_____

_____

_____

_____

_____

_____

_____

_____

_____

_____

_____

_____

_____

_____

Activity:

As I mentioned earlier, going through a divorce can feel like being stuck in a tornado. If you do not find other things to focus on, it can suck you in and keep you twirling until the end when it spits you out. Now, you might be thinking that you will throw yourself into work, you will concentrate on your children, you will finally reconnect with family and that all these things will be enough to keep you sane and in the proper mindset, but I assure you they are not enough. All the aspects of your life I listed are aspects of your married life. I am asking you to find YOU as separate and apart from your marriage, and all the different roles you play as a married individual.

I am a true fan of the show Blue Bloods on ABC. I mean, who does not love Tom Selleck? During the premier of Season 8, we learn that a character's wife had passed away. This character, Detective Danny Reagan, throws himself into his work as a NYPD detective and his entire family is trying to make him realize that if he focuses on his children, he will be ok. Also, during the episode we witness his talks with his therapist. However, neither work, nor therapy, nor focusing on his children are helping him get over the loss of his wife. All I could think about is how a divorce is the loss of a marriage, a way of life, and can seem like a death of sorts. In fact, most studies that list the top 10 causes of stress list the first as being the death of a love one and the second being divorce.

If I were Detective Reagan's best friend, solely based on my years of experience as a counselor helping people get through the loss of their loved ones due to divorce, I would have recommended that in combination with his other coping mechanisms, that he find some activity that challenges and interests him to occupy those moments when he feels like he is getting sucked into the funnel of loss. As I previously mentioned, you must grieve loss in order to move past it, but you have to combine that grief with positive actions to make it through.

Think about one (or more) activities you can start that will keep your mind off the divorce. Activities provide you with a much-needed escape from the tornado. Have you always wanted to learn a new language? Well, now is the time to start. Have you been meaning to join a gym but never got to it? It's a perfect time to get in shape before the beginning of a new chapter in your life. Did you want to learn how to crochet, ride a bike, run a marathon, or any other activity you have been putting off? Now is the time to dive into it and use it as a break from the craziness that will run your life for a while. I can imagine what you are thinking: *how am I possibly going to fit an activity or new hobby into my already chaotic life?* There is always time for you if you make it. I urge you that there is no time like the present to make time for You!

Also, I would suggest that you form a practice of meditation in addition to any activity you choose. When we are tense, we forget to breathe, and when we forget to breathe, we are tense. It's a vicious cycle. Pick a time each day, whether it be early in the morning before the kids wake up, during your lunch break at work, or after everyone in the house goes to bed and clear your mind. Meditation can give you a chance to breathe and feel renewed. There are plenty of apps you can download on your phone that guide you through meditation. There are many forms of meditation and most do not take very long or much effort on your part. Every biography of every successful person I have ever read mentions that they meditate as a crucial part of the proper mindset toward success. That is the goal here, right? We want the divorce process to be successful in every aspect, especially your mental health and well-being during the process and at the end of it all.

Finally, with regard to this category, an activity is reliable. It is something you can plan into your week, look forward to, and rely on. Things may seem like they are falling apart from time to time during the divorce process, and they may seem out of your control or not going as planned. However, if you find an activity you enjoy and do it daily or weekly throughout the process, it will be the one thing you can count on that will bring you happiness, joy, and be there for you after the process is over as well. It is important to feel this way and look forward to things so that you do not become depressed and/or potentially develop self-destructive habits and dependencies, such as turning to drugs or alcohol. If you keep yourself busy, happy and engaged in positive activities, the whole process just will not seem as bad or as long.

NOTES:

_____

_____

_____

_____

_____

_____

_____

_____

_____

_____

_____

_____

Helen M. Dukhan, Esq., LL.M

TYING IT ALL UP

So, there you have it. You have the steps you need to prepare yourself for divorce. If you put your trust in me, in my experience, and the fact that I truly want everyone who has to go through divorce to run around after everything is said and done screaming "Nothing Says a Good Day Like a Divorce!", and follow the steps I have given you, you will truly reap the benefits and value of this guide and save yourself time and money, lessen your stress levels, and hopefully have an advantage over the outcome of your divorce.

Sounds easy, right? NO! It is not an easy process, and it is not easy to get prepared, but as Thomas Roosevelt famously once said, "Nothing in the world is worth having or worth doing unless it means effort, pain, difficulty… I have never in my life envied a human being who led an easy life. I have envied a great many people who led difficult lives and led them well."

That is my goal in writing this guide for you. I hope that even though you are about to embark on a difficult season of your life, that despite the difficulty, you still live that part of your life and those years that follow well.

If you Get Organized, Gain Access to Funds, Form a Support Team, and Develop a Proper Mindset, according to the information and suggestions in this guide, I am confident, and you should be too, that you will be ready and you will succeed as a result of all your effort.

There are some other things that you should think about when starting the divorce process that are not crucial to getting prepared for divorce, but that I hope you consider. I discuss those "Additional Things to Consider" in the pages that follow this conclusion. I hope you will review them and that they help you finalize your plans for divorce.

I wish you nothing but the best in your journey. I love nothing more then hearing from people who have utilized my step-by-step guide to prepare for their own divorce, whether the feedback is positive or not. I hope to someday update this guide based on all the feedback I receive from readers like you. So, please email any comments, suggestions, reviews, thoughts, anything (even if the body of the email just screams: "NOTHING SAYS A GOOD DAY LIKE A DIVORCE!") to Dukhan@hdfamilylaw.com. I look forward to hearing from you.

ADDITIONAL THINGS TO CONSIDER

PLAN HOW YOU WILL DELIVER THE NEWS:

If you are the initiator, you should deliver the news once you are well on your way to completing all the steps in this guide. Let's assume you are organized, have access to funds, have built the start of your support system, including having hired an attorney, and are well on your way to the proper mindset. You should discuss with your attorney the proper time to deliver the news to your spouse, if they still do not know, and the proper way to do it.

Occasionally, my client and I decide that simply serving the spouse is best. Many considerations go into this decision because blindsiding someone with divorce is probably not the very best way to go about it. In most circumstances, we have the documents already filed when my client speaks to the spouse about their intentions. We give the spouse a bit of time to process and then we serve them in a few days or a week or whenever the client decides it is time. The reason that we file the initial divorce documents prior to the client discussing their intentions with their spouse is at that point the client is protected if the spouse decides to suddenly transfer funds, or dissipate assets, or somehow disturb the status quo. By filing we let the court know our intentions to get a divorce and both the client and spouse are not to disrupt any accounts, assets, properties, or other holdings without consent of the other or without the court's permission.

NOTES:

_____

_____

_____

_____

_____

_____

_____

_____

_____

_____

_____

_____

_____

_____

_____

_____

_____

_____

_____

Nothing Says a Good Day Like a DIVORCE If You Prepare for it!

_____

_____

_____

_____

_____

_____

_____

_____

_____

_____

_____

_____

_____

_____

_____

_____

_____

_____

_____

_____

_____

PLAN FOR THE KIDS:

Often times, the parents are still living under the same roof when one files for divorce and during much of the divorce process. Therefore, discussing plans for the kids (custody & parenting time) does not seem like a top priority. However, forming a parenting plan for the children at the outset of the case and figuring out the details of the plan that are acceptable to both parents as early on in the divorce process as possible will inevitably save you a ton of money and reduce stress.

Almost every state bases their custody decisions on a standard of what is in the "Best Interest of the Child". Each state has a list of factors they go by to determine what is in the best interest of the child. Moreover, each state has their own age at which a child is considered mature enough and able to decide their own fate, or at least state their opinion.

Your attorney should counsel you as to what your state's preference is when it comes to child custody and visitation. Your attorney should explain to you the difference between legal custody (decision making) and physical custody (which parent the child lives with). You should also discuss whether your state prefers joint decision-making or sole decision-making and what your state deems as a standard parenting time/visitation schedule. With your attorney's advice, you will be able to decide what a reasonable plan would be based on the laws and standards of your State as applied to your family's unique dynamic and circumstances.

In cases where the parents differ on their ideas of custody and parenting time and the court needs more guidance, they can appoint a guardian for the child. Some states appoint an attorney to represent the child, and some states have organizations comprised of psychologists, social workers, or other trained professionals to perform a custody evaluation of the family and provide their own recommendations. However helpful these methods are for ultimately deciding who should have custody and who should have parenting time, I believe there is no one better suited to decide such decisions than the parents themselves. If the parents can set aside their emotions and think rationally and logically about the child, their future, and each other, they can in most instances come to such decisions without the assistance of third parties who really know nothing about them or their family.

Again, the earlier in the process you discuss this and are able to negotiate a proper parenting plan agreement, the better off your children will be, the better of your sanity will be, and the better off your wallet will be.

It is my hope that this section gives you the tools you need to ask your attorney the proper questions, do your own research, and be armed with the knowledge of at the least what you should be thinking about and considering when having to deal with such crucial, sensitive, and private decisions.

NOTES:

_____

_____

_____

_____

_____

_____

_____

_____

_____

_____

_____

_____

_____

_____

_____

_____

Nothing Says a Good Day Like a DIVORCE If You Prepare for it!

COMMUNICATION DURING DIVORCE:

Whether you have come to the point of deciding to get a divorce, or have found out that your spouse has decided to file for divorce — or worse has already filed without discussing it with you first, more often than not there are many emotions flying around such as anger, resentment, sadness, and event hate. A lot of individuals who come in to my office have no communication with their spouse. Many men and women whom I represent no longer live together and the only communication between them is yelling at each other and arguing about everything. Many times, by the time the divorce is decided upon, the relationship has completely broken down, thereby freezing any meaningful communication between the spouses. However, most divorcing couples have children and issues that they need to communicate about. In these circumstances, I often suggest a few options that can be used either individually, or in concert with one another, such as:

Neutral Third-Party Intermediary:

You and your spouse may decide upon an individual who would be willing to be a go-between and pass along communication between the two of you. This is not an individual who is trying to help you work things out or settle your issues. Rather, this person is simply someone whom you are both willing to speak to, whom you both trust, and whom assists you in communicating. If you and your spouse have decided on a visitation schedule and/or parenting plan and cannot stand the sight of each other, this person can also be the person who transports the children or is a pick up and drop off point between the two of you.

Communication Tools:

Utilize one of the many possible communication tools for co-parents. There are many such tools you can look up online to use for calendaring and communicating. Some you have to pay for, and some are free. Some such tools are:

a. Talking Parent

b. Cozi

c. Google Calendar

d. Our Family Wizard

e. Coparently

f. Support pay

g. squarehub

h. 2houses

i. isplit

I want to make it very clear that I do not suggest or prefer any of the above tools. I am not sponsored by any of the mentioned tools and do not know the effectiveness of any of them or endorse the use of any of them. I am merely pointing out that they are available. There are many more apps and tools and I suggest you do your own research and seek out reviews and recommendations before choosing the right one(s) for you. Many of the above-mentioned communication tools are for different purposes: some for parenting, some for paying child support and other expenses, and some for dividing assets without having to communicate or be in the same place with the other spouse.

Again, I can't emphasize enough that if you and your spouse cannot personally communicate and choose one of these options, you must take emotion out of the communication and out of your decision making. This can be very challenging. I often urge my clients to cease using social media during their divorce. Much litigation has surrounded the use of social media against spouses in divorce cases, and it can come in as evidence against you, even if the other spouse obtained the information by using a friend or breaking into your account. I often urge my clients to stop posting on Facebook, Twitter, Instagram, or any other source of social media during the divorce, even if the post has nothing to do with the other party or the divorce. Therefore, using communication tools can be risky if you do not remove the emotional aspect of your communications and strictly limit use of the tools for the purposes for which they are intended.

Attorneys:

If your spouse is unrepresented by an attorney, then your attorney can freely communicate with your spouse. However, many attorneys do not prefer this method of communication because of the appearance of impropriety and plus it is very difficult to communicate with an unrepresented individual. Understandably so, an unrepresented individual is defensive and does not trust or want to communicate with the other spouse's attorney. Also, an unrepresented person does not know the law, and they do not know their realistic options and what a realistic outcome looks like. Therefore, their demands are often unrealistic and purely emotional.

If you and your spouse are both represented, you can communicate through your attorneys. I often do all the communicating for my clients through letters and phone calls to the other spouse's attorney. However, I must caution you that this road is very costly. The clients who choose this route are often high net worth clients who can afford this service, but most find a different option to use for communication with their spouse.

I always encourage communication between spouses. However, if that is absolutely out of the question, I encourage them to utilize one of the options above or find other creative options to communicate and work toward a settlement of their case.

NOTES:

_____

_____

_____

_____

_____

_____

_____

_____

_____

_____

_____

_____

_____

_____

_____

_____

_____

_____

HEALTH COVERAGE:

You must plan for the fact that once the divorce is finalized, you will not be able to stay under your spouse's employer-sponsored health care coverage. You will be able to stay under a private insurance plan, if those are the terms of the agreement, but not under employer-provided plans.

After your divorce is finalized, you may be able to temporarily keep your coverage through "COBRA". It is my understanding that if your spouse's employer has 20 or more employees, COBRA allows you to continue coverage for up to 36 months. However, your spouse will not have to pay for you to continue coverage and will not have to pay for you to obtain private health insurance coverage. I suggest you research COBRA insurance to better equip you in case you need to utilize it.

The Affordable Healthcare Act is another option for those needing insurance. The Act provides many subsidies and health care options. Of course, this option depends on the administration and if it is still exists. If such benefits are still available definitely consider it.

This should be discussed between you and your attorney. Also, it should be decided who will cover the children under their health insurance coverage and how the premiums, deductibles, co-pays, and unreimbursed medical expenses will be paid for.

NOTES:

_____

_____

_____

_____

_____

_____

_____

_____

_____

_____

_____

_____

_____

_____

_____

_____

_____

_____

_____

NO GUARANTEES:

You should be very wary of any attorney or professional who makes guarantees about the outcome of your divorce or the outcome of any decision you make. There is no way to guarantee any aspect of the divorce process. Much is left up to the court's decision, the law as applied to the facts, and the gray space in- between the black and white areas of your family dynamics.

I have had many individuals explain to me that their previous attorney guaranteed they would be awarded legal fees, and they were not. Sometimes they tell me that the attorney guaranteed they would get full custody of the children, and they did not. For example, one attorney, by consistently making arguments against the other spouse in pursuit of full custody for his client, made it seem as if his client was alienating the other parent; his client lost some of the time he would have otherwise had with his child. I had to do my best to clean up the mess his attorney made and ended up being able to settle on a parenting plan that suited both my client and the spouse. I did so by managing expectations and amicably working with the other attorney on a reasonable outcome rather than by attacking the other spouse.

As my previously-mentioned blog post discusses, do not seek an attorney known as a "Shark". Rather, seek an attorney who will protect your best interests while managing your expectations. Of course, you do not want a wallflower incapable or unwilling to stand up and fight for your rights, but you also do not want someone who consistently upsets the court, the other spouse, and the other attorney. More often than not, that same attorney upsets every professional who is employed to help in the case, and the results do not go your way solely for the fact that no one can handle that attorney's personality. In essence, do not hire an attorney who seems like they may end up doing you a great disservice with their "shark" like habits.

NOTES:

_____

_____

_____

_____

_____

_____

_____

_____

_____

_____

Nothing Says a Good Day Like a DIVORCE If You Prepare for it!

ALTERNATIVES TO TRADITIONAL LITIGATION:

You should be aware of the alternatives to traditional litigation. Based upon your review of the alternatives, you should weigh your options and decide what you believe is best for you. On a side note, even if you think mediation is best, if your spouse does not agree or does not want to go through mediation, you will be forced by the court to go the traditional litigation route to get a divorce. However, whether you both decide to mediate or choose the traditional litigation route, it is imperative to be represented by an attorney. If you both decide to go through mediation, your attorney will be a consultant for you; they will review any agreements, proposals and help you negotiate for what is best for you. Either way, if you want an amicable resolution of your divorce, it is extremely important for you to find an attorney who believes in alternatives to conventional litigation and supports negotiation between you and your spouse without the attorney's involvement. The attorney who supports an amicable settlement and values settlement will negotiate on your behalf as much as possible to avoid needless litigation.

As I mentioned before, no one knows what is best for you and your family other than you and your spouse. Therefore, while an attorney should guide you, counsel you, provide you with options, and give you their expert advice, no one should be in control of the ultimate outcome of your divorce other than you and your spouse. The judge in the black robe does not know you and does not know your spouse, and they are bound to act pursuant to the laws and boundaries as set by statute. Regardless of the method decided upon, or what fictional stories people tell, no one wins in a divorce. That is why it is strongly suggested that you, your spouse, and the attorneys representing you both, be as creative as possible to settle every issue so both of you leave satisfied, because the reality is neither of you will leave the marriage receiving 100% of what you hoped for. Therefore, if you find an attorney who does not support mediation and negotiation, you will be tied to litigation and wasting money you may not need to spend.

Litigation is extremely expensive. Litigation involves much preparation, lengthy conferences, lengthy court appearances, much effort on behalf of the attorney, and much expert involvement that you and your spouse will have to fund. Also, even if you have unlimited funds, litigation will typically destroy any semblance of respect, or at the very least tolerance, either one of you has towards the other. So, I urge you to strongly consider the alternatives that are described below.

Mediation:

You and your spouse meet with a neutral third party, the mediator, who is experienced in assisting the both of you while you work through the issues you need to resolve. Mediation is done with an eye toward an amicable divorce. The mediator may be an attorney or simply a professional who is experienced and trained to perform mediation. The mediator is objective, not taking either side.

People think of mediation as a cost-effective approach. Although, I'm not sure people realize what is meant by cost-effective. Most mediators that I recommend are divorce attorneys and charge as much per hour as any other divorce attorney. Most mediators I recommend who are worth the money require the parties to have attorneys represent them so that the parties are aware of their options and make educated decisions based on the attorney's knowledge of the law and all possible outcomes. The mediator, even if they are an attorney, cannot provide individual legal advice to either of the spouses. Therefore, in my opinion, it is imperative to hire an attorney and have the attorney suggest mediators. So, how does a mediator save money?

Mediation can save you and your spouse money by guiding you toward a settlement. Therefore, you have more of a chance of avoiding costly litigation in court, motion practice, and ultimately a trial to decide key issues. The value of going through mediation is really that the mediator fosters meaningful communication between the spouses — maybe the first meaningful communication they have had in years — and the spouses get to decide the issues of your divorce.

NOTES:

_____

_____

_____

_____

_____

_____

_____

_____

_____

_____

_____

_____

_____

_____

Arbitration:

Arbitration is another option when getting divorced. Often, people who cannot settle their issues but want to remain out of the courtroom and keep their issues as private as possible choose this option.

Arbitration is a hearing, a trial, held in a private setting before an arbitrator. Arbitrators are often retired judges or very experienced attorneys. Arbitrations are scheduled on dates and times convenient to all the parties involved, unlike court trials, which are scheduled when the court has time.

Unlike having a trial in court where you are bound by court's timeline, rules, and procedures, in arbitration the divorcing couple with the guidance of their attorneys can define what procedures will be followed and how long the arbitrator will have to render their decision.

One major difference between arbitration and mediation is that any agreement made during mediation is not binding until the formal agreement is signed and/or put on the record, whereas any decision made by an arbitrator is binding. In fact, any decision made by an arbitrator cannot be appealed, unlike a decision made by a judge after trial.

In my opinion, arbitration is risky, but suitable for some. Considering you have completed, or are well on your way to completing the steps above, you should have formed your support team as led by your divorce attorney, and your attorney should let you know if they recommend arbitration as an option you should consider.

NOTES:

_____

_____

_____

_____

_____

_____

_____

_____

_____

_____

_____

_____

_____

_____

Negotiation:

I have mentioned before that in my experience it is imperative for both spouses to have attorneys that believe in meaningful negotiations and are good at it. You can automatically sense if an attorney values settlement by the words they use. For example, I explain to most of my divorce clients where I believe settlement is possible that negotiating a proper settlement is best for everyone involved. I often pride myself on being able to settle cases that would otherwise seem to be the most litigious and complicated without ever sacrificing my client's goals and wishes. However, due to those that refused to settle or had issues that were not appropriate for settlement, I have represented clients through many trials. As a result, I have witnessed what trials do to families and the tens of thousands of dollars they cost, and therefore I believe that settlement should be everyone's priority, if possible.

Negotiation is not considered an alternative to divorce litigation, but by having two attorneys that value settlement, through negotiation the parties are given the opportunity to decide issues of child custody, child visitation, child support, alimony and division of assets, for themselves.

In conclusion, with regard to alternatives to divorce litigation, it is important to take note that while a judge's decision may be fair to both parties, it is impossible for a judge to take into account the specific needs of either party. To the contrary, if you choose to mediate, arbitrate, negotiate, or to go through any other collaborative law options not listed in this guide, it is possible to find creative solutions to each issue which accurately reflects your family's specific needs without having to spend all of your money.

NOTES:

_____

_____

_____

_____

_____

_____

_____

_____

_____

_____

_____

_____

_____

_____

_____

CLOSING REMARKS NOTHING SAYS A GOOD DAY LIKE A DIVORCE

CONGRATULATIONS!! If you are reading this page you are well on your way, or have achieved, your right to run around screaming to everyone you meet, "NOTHING SAYS A GOOD DAY LIKE A DIVORCE!!!!!" As a seasoned divorce attorney in New York and New Jersey, I can honestly say that you are a champion for taking advantage of this guide for the courage and effort it took to get through it, and for your determination to get it done right.

While there is never a one-size-fits-all solution to the process of divorce, it is my sincere hope that this guide helped you prepare for your divorce, accept your divorce, and get to the other side courageously and successfully.

It is also my hope that if this book was of value to you, and helped you succeed in protecting your sanity, money, time, family, and your future, that you will let any friends, family, or individuals you meet along your journey going through or preparing to go through divorce know it!! I wrote this guide in hopes that it will reach as many people as possible who need the guidance and information contained in this guide. Please do your part in helping my dream come true and pass this Guide along so that it will continuously help those in need of what I believe is the most valuable process to gaining the advantage necessary at the outset of any divorce.

This is your new beginning. I hope that your future will be bright, free, and full of love and success in all your new endeavors!

Helen M. Dukhan

NOTES:

NOTES:

_____

_____

_____

_____

_____

_____

_____

_____

_____

_____

_____

_____

_____

_____

_____

_____

_____

_____

Made in the USA
Columbia, SC
14 July 2019